The Poetry of Henry Wadsworth Longfellow

Volume III – Voices of the Night

Index of Index

The Warning
HENRY WADSWORTH LONGFELLOW – A SHORT BIOGRAPHY
HENRY WADSWORTH LONGFELLOW – A CONCISE BIBLIOGRAPHY

VOICES OF THE NIGHT

PRELUDE

Pleasant it was, when woods were green,
And winds were soft and low,
To lie amid some sylvan scene.
Where, the long drooping boughs between,
Shadows dark and sunlight sheen
Alternate come and go;

Or where the denser grove receives
No sunlight from above,
But the dark foliage interweaves
In one unbroken roof of leaves,
Underneath whose sloping eaves
The shadows hardly move.

Beneath some patriarchal tree
I lay upon the ground;
His hoary arms uplifted he,
And all the broad leaves over me
Clapped their little hands in glee,
With one continuous sound;—

A slumberous sound, a sound that brings
The feelings of a dream,
As of innumerable wings,
As, when a bell no longer swings,
Faint the hollow murmur rings
O'er meadow, lake, and stream.

And dreams of that which cannot die,
Bright visions, came to me,
As lapped in thought I used to lie,
And gaze into the summer sky,
Where the sailing clouds went by,
Like ships upon the sea;

Dreams that the soul of youth engage
Ere Fancy has been quelled;

Old legends of the monkish page,
Traditions of the saint and sage,
Tales that have the rime of age,
And chronicles of Eld.

And, loving still these quaint old themes,
Even in the city's throng
I feel the freshness of the streams,
That, crossed by shades and sunny gleams,
Water the green land of dreams,
The holy land of song.

Therefore, at Pentecost, which brings
The Spring, clothed like a bride,
When nestling buds unfold their wings,
And bishop's-caps have golden rings,
Musing upon many things,
I sought the woodlands wide.

The green trees whispered low and mild;
It was a sound of joy!
They were my playmates when a child,
And rocked me in their arms so wild!
Still they looked at me and smiled,
As if I were a boy;

And ever whispered, mild and low,
"Come, be a child once more!"
And waved their long arms to and fro,
And beckoned solemnly and slow;
O, I could not choose but go
Into the woodlands hoar,—

Into the blithe and breathing air,
Into the solemn wood,
Solemn and silent everywhere
Nature with folded hands seemed there
Kneeling at her evening prayer!
Like one in prayer I stood.

Before me rose an avenue
Of tall and sombrous pines;
Abroad their fan-like branches grew,
And, where the sunshine darted through,
Spread a vapor soft and blue,
In long and sloping lines.

And, falling on my weary brain,

Like a fast-falling shower,
The dreams of youth came back again,
Low lispings of the summer rain,
Dropping on the ripened grain,
As once upon the flower.

Visions of childhood! Stay, O stay!
Ye were so sweet and wild!
And distant voices seemed to say,
"It cannot be! They pass away!
Other themes demand thy lay;
Thou art no more a child!

"The land of Song within thee lies,
Watered by living springs;
The lids of Fancy's sleepless eyes
Are gates unto that Paradise,
Holy thoughts, like stars, arise,
Its clouds are angels' wings.

"Learn, that henceforth thy song shall be,
Not mountains capped with snow,
Nor forests sounding like the sea,
Nor rivers flowing ceaselessly,
Where the woodlands bend to see
The bending heavens below.

"There is a forest where the din
Of iron branches sounds!
A mighty river roars between,
And whosoever looks therein
Sees the heavens all black with sin,
Sees not its depths, nor bounds.

"Athwart the swinging branches cast,
Soft rays of sunshine pour;
Then comes the fearful wintry blast
Our hopes, like withered leaves, fail fast;
Pallid lips say, 'It is past!
We can return no more!,

"Look, then, into thine heart, and write!
Yes, into Life's deep stream!
All forms of sorrow and delight,
All solemn Voices of the Night,
That can soothe thee, or affright,—
Be these henceforth thy theme."

HYMN TO THE NIGHT

I heard the trailing garments of the Night
Sweep through her marble halls!
I saw her sable skirts all fringed with light
From the celestial walls!

I felt her presence, by its spell of might,
Stoop o'er me from above;
The calm, majestic presence of the Night,
As of the one I love.

I heard the sounds of sorrow and delight,
The manifold, soft chimes,
That fill the haunted chambers of the Night
Like some old poet's rhymes.

From the cool cisterns of the midnight air
My spirit drank repose;
The fountain of perpetual peace flows there,—
From those deep cisterns flows.

O holy Night! from thee I learn to bear
What man has borne before!
Thou layest thy finger on the lips of Care,
And they complain no more.

Peace! Peace! Orestes-like I breathe this prayer!
Descend with broad-winged flight,
The welcome, the thrice-prayed for, the most fair,
The best-beloved Night!

A PSALM OF LIFE

WHAT THE HEART OF THE YOUNG MAN SAID TO THE PSALMIST

Tell me not, in mournful numbers,
Life is but an empty dream!
For the soul is dead that slumbers,
And things are not what they seem.

Life is real! Life is earnest!
And the grave is not its goal;
Dust thou art, to dust returnest,

Was not spoken of the soul.

Not enjoyment, and not sorrow,
Is our destined end or way;
But to act, that each to-morrow
Find us farther than to-day.

Art is long, and Time is fleeting,
And our hearts, though stout and brave,
Still, like muffled drums, are beating
Funeral marches to the grave.

In the world's broad field of battle,
In the bivouac of Life,
Be not like dumb, driven cattle!
Be a hero in the strife!

Trust no Future, howe'er pleasant!
Let the dead Past bury its dead!
Act,—act in the living Present!
Heart within, and God o'erhead!

Lives of great men all remind us
We can make our lives sublime,
And, departing, leave behind us
Footprints on the sands of time;—

Footprints, that perhaps another,
Sailing o'er life's solemn main,
A forlorn and shipwrecked brother,
Seeing, shall take heart again.

Let us, then, be up and doing,
With a heart for any fate;
Still achieving, still pursuing,
Learn to labor and to wait.

THE REAPER AND THE FLOWERS

There is a Reaper, whose name is Death,
And, with his sickle keen,
He reaps the bearded grain at a breath,
And the flowers that grow between.

"Shall I have naught that is fair?" saith he;
"Have naught but the bearded grain?

Though the breath of these flowers is sweet to me,
I will give them all back again."

He gazed at the flowers with tearful eyes,
He kissed their drooping leaves;
It was for the Lord of Paradise
He bound them in his sheaves.

"My Lord has need of these flowerets gay,"
The Reaper said, and smiled;
"Dear tokens of the earth are they,
Where he was once a child.

"They shall all bloom in fields of light,
Transplanted by my care,
And saints, upon their garments white,
These sacred blossoms wear."

And the mother gave, in tears and pain,
The flowers she most did love;
She knew she should find them all again
In the fields of light above.

O, not in cruelty, not in wrath,
The Reaper came that day;
'T was an angel visited the green earth,
And took the flowers away.

THE LIGHT OF STARS

The night is come, but not too soon;
And sinking silently,
All silently, the little moon
Drops down behind the sky.

There is no light in earth or heaven
But the cold light of stars;
And the first watch of night is given
To the red planet Mars.

Is it the tender star of love?
The star of love and dreams?
O no! from that blue tent above,
A hero's armor gleams.

And earnest thoughts within me rise,

When I behold afar,
Suspended in the evening skies,
The shield of that red star.

O star of strength! I see thee stand
And smile upon my pain;
Thou beckonest with thy mailed hand,
And I am strong again.

Within my breast there is no light
But the cold light of stars;
I give the first watch of the night
To the red planet Mars.

The star of the unconquered will,
He rises in my breast,
Serene, and resolute, and still,
And calm, and self-possessed.

And thou, too, whosoe'er thou art,
That readest this brief psalm,
As one by one thy hopes depart,
Be resolute and calm.

O fear not in a world like this,
And thou shalt know erelong,
Know how sublime a thing it is
To suffer and be strong.

FOOTSTEPS OF ANGELS

When the hours of Day are numbered,
And the voices of the Night
Wake the better soul, that slumbered,
To a holy, calm delight;

Ere the evening lamps are lighted,
And, like phantoms grim and tall,
Shadows from the fitful firelight
Dance upon the parlor wall;

Then the forms of the departed
Enter at the open door;
The beloved, the true-hearted,
Come to visit me once more;

He, the young and strong, who cherished
Noble longings for the strife,
By the roadside fell and perished,
Weary with the march of life!

They, the holy ones and weakly,
Who the cross of suffering bore,
Folded their pale hands so meekly,
Spake with us on earth no more!

And with them the Being Beauteous,
Who unto my youth was given,
More than all things else to love me,
And is now a saint in heaven.

With a slow and noiseless footstep
Comes that messenger divine,
Takes the vacant chair beside me,
Lays her gentle hand in mine.

And she sits and gazes at me
With those deep and tender eyes,
Like the stars, so still and saint-like,
Looking downward from the skies.

Uttered not, yet comprehended,
Is the spirit's voiceless prayer,
Soft rebukes, in blessings ended,
Breathing from her lips of air.

Oh, though oft depressed and lonely,
All my fears are laid aside,
If I but remember only
Such as these have lived and died!

FLOWERS

Spake full well, in language quaint and olden,
One who dwelleth by the castled Rhine,
When he called the flowers, so blue and golden,
Stars, that in earth's firmament do shine.

Stars they are, wherein we read our history,
As astrologers and seers of eld;
Yet not wrapped about with awful mystery,
Like the burning stars, which they beheld.

Wondrous truths, and manifold as wondrous,
God hath written in those stars above;
But not less in the bright flowerets under us
Stands the revelation of his love.

Bright and glorious is that revelation,
Written all over this great world of ours;
Making evident our own creation,
In these stars of earth, these golden flowers.

And the Poet, faithful and far-seeing,
Sees, alike in stars and flowers, a part
Of the self-same, universal being,
Which is throbbing in his brain and heart.

Gorgeous flowerets in the sunlight shining,
Blossoms flaunting in the eye of day,
Tremulous leaves, with soft and silver lining,
Buds that open only to decay;

Brilliant hopes, all woven in gorgeous tissues,
Flaunting gayly in the golden light;
Large desires, with most uncertain issues,
Tender wishes, blossoming at night!

These in flowers and men are more than seeming;
Workings are they of the self-same powers,
Which the Poet, in no idle dreaming,
Seeth in himself and in the flowers.

Everywhere about us are they glowing,
Some like stars, to tell us Spring is born;
Others, their blue eyes with tears o'er-flowing,
Stand like Ruth amid the golden corn;

Not alone in Spring's armorial bearing,
And in Summer's green-emblazoned field,
But in arms of brave old Autumn's wearing,
In the centre of his brazen shield;

Not alone in meadows and green alleys,
On the mountain-top, and by the brink
Of sequestered pools in woodland valleys,
Where the slaves of nature stoop to drink;

Not alone in her vast dome of glory,
Not on graves of bird and beast alone,

But in old cathedrals, high and hoary,
On the tombs of heroes, carved in stone;

In the cottage of the rudest peasant,
In ancestral homes, whose crumbling towers,
Speaking of the Past unto the Present,
Tell us of the ancient Games of Flowers;

In all places, then, and in all seasons,
Flowers expand their light and soul-like wings,
Teaching us, by most persuasive reasons,
How akin they are to human things.

And with childlike, credulous affection
We behold their tender buds expand;
Emblems of our own great resurrection,
Emblems of the bright and better land.

THE BELEAGUERED CITY

I have read, in some old, marvellous tale,
Some legend strange and vague,
That a midnight host of spectres pale
Beleaguered the walls of Prague.

Beside the Moldau's rushing stream,
With the wan moon overhead,
There stood, as in an awful dream,
The army of the dead.

White as a sea-fog, landward bound,
The spectral camp was seen,
And, with a sorrowful, deep sound,
The river flowed between.

No other voice nor sound was there,
No drum, nor sentry's pace;
The mist-like banners clasped the air,
As clouds with clouds embrace.

But when the old cathedral bell
Proclaimed the morning prayer,
The white pavilions rose and fell
On the alarmed air.

Down the broad valley fast and far

The troubled army fled;
Up rose the glorious morning star,
The ghastly host was dead.

I have read, in the marvellous heart of man,
That strange and mystic scroll,
That an army of phantoms vast and wan
Beleaguer the human soul.

Encamped beside Life's rushing stream,
In Fancy's misty light,
Gigantic shapes and shadows gleam
Portentous through the night.

Upon its midnight battle-ground
The spectral camp is seen,
And, with a sorrowful, deep sound,
Flows the River of Life between.

No other voice nor sound is there,
In the army of the grave;
No other challenge breaks the air,
But the rushing of Life's wave.

And when the solemn and deep churchbell
Entreats the soul to pray,
The midnight phantoms feel the spell,
The shadows sweep away.

Down the broad Vale of Tears afar
The spectral camp is fled;
Faith shineth as a morning star,
Our ghastly fears are dead.

MIDNIGHT MASS FOR THE DYING YEAR

Yes, the Year is growing old,
And his eye is pale and bleared!
Death, with frosty hand and cold,
Plucks the old man by the beard,
Sorely, sorely!

The leaves are falling, falling,
Solemnly and slow;
Caw! caw! the rooks are calling,
It is a sound of woe,

A sound of woe!

Through woods and mountain passes
The winds, like anthems, roll;
They are chanting solemn masses,
Singing, "Pray for this poor soul,
Pray, pray!"

And the hooded clouds, like friars,
Tell their beads in drops of rain,
And patter their doleful prayers;
But their prayers are all in vain,
All in vain!

There he stands in the foul weather,
The foolish, fond Old Year,
Crowned with wild flowers and with heather,
Like weak, despised Lear,
A king, a king!

Then comes the summer-like day,
Bids the old man rejoice!
His joy! his last! O, the man gray
Loveth that ever-soft voice,
Gentle and low.

To the crimson woods he saith,
To the voice gentle and low
Of the soft air, like a daughter's breath,
"Pray do not mock me so!
Do not laugh at me!"

And now the sweet day is dead;
Cold in his arms it lies;
No stain from its breath is spread
Over the glassy skies,
No mist or stain!

Then, too, the Old Year dieth,
And the forests utter a moan,
Like the voice of one who crieth
In the wilderness alone,
"Vex not his ghost!"

Then comes, with an awful roar,
Gathering and sounding on,
The storm-wind from Labrador,
The wind Euroclydon,

The storm-wind!

Howl! howl! and from the forest
Sweep the red leaves away!
Would, the sins that thou abhorrest,
O Soul! could thus decay,
And be swept away!
For there shall come a mightier blast,
There shall be a darker day;

And the stars, from heaven down-cast
Like red leaves be swept away!
Kyrie, eleyson!
Christe, eleyson!

EARLIER POEMS

AN APRIL DAY

When the warm sun, that brings
Seed-time and harvest, has returned again,
'T is sweet to visit the still wood, where springs
The first flower of the plain.

I love the season well,
When forest glades are teeming with bright forms,
Nor dark and many-folded clouds foretell
The coming-on of storms.

From the earth's loosened mould
The sapling draws its sustenance, and thrives;
Though stricken to the heart with winter's cold,
The drooping tree revives.

The softly-warbled song
Comes from the pleasant woods, and colored wings
Glance quick in the bright sun, that moves along
The forest openings.

When the bright sunset fills
The silver woods with light, the green slope throws
Its shadows in the hollows of the hills,
And wide the upland glows.

And when the eve is born,
In the blue lake the sky, o'er-reaching far,

Is hollowed out and the moon dips her horn,
And twinkles many a star.

Inverted in the tide
Stand the gray rocks, and trembling shadows throw,
And the fair trees look over, side by side,
And see themselves below.

Sweet April! many a thought
Is wedded unto thee, as hearts are wed;
Nor shall they fail, till, to its autumn brought,
Life's golden fruit is shed.

AUTUMN

With what a glory comes and goes the year!
The buds of spring, those beautiful harbingers
Of sunny skies and cloudless times, enjoy
Life's newness, and earth's garniture spread out;
And when the silver habit of the clouds
Comes down upon the autumn sun, and with
A sober gladness the old year takes up
His bright inheritance of golden fruits,
A pomp and pageant fill the splendid scene.

There is a beautiful spirit breathing now
Its mellow richness on the clustered trees,
And, from a beaker full of richest dyes,
Pouring new glory on the autumn woods,
And dipping in warm light the pillared clouds.
Morn on the mountain, like a summer bird,
Lifts up her purple wing, and in the vales
The gentle wind, a sweet and passionate wooer,
Kisses the blushing leaf, and stirs up life
Within the solemn woods of ash deep-crimsoned,
And silver beech, and maple yellow-leaved,
Where Autumn, like a faint old man, sits down
By the wayside a-weary. Through the trees
The golden robin moves. The purple finch,
That on wild cherry and red cedar feeds,
A winter bird, comes with its plaintive whistle,
And pecks by the witch-hazel, whilst aloud
From cottage roofs the warbling blue-bird sings,
And merrily, with oft-repeated stroke,
Sounds from the threshing-floor the busy flail.

O what a glory doth this world put on
For him who, with a fervent heart, goes forth
Under the bright and glorious sky, and looks
On duties well performed, and days well spent!
For him the wind, ay, and the yellow leaves,
Shall have a voice, and give him eloquent teachings.
He shall so hear the solemn hymn that Death
Has lifted up for all, that he shall go
To his long resting-place without a tear.

WOODS IN WINTER

When winter winds are piercing chill,
And through the hawthorn blows the gale,
With solemn feet I tread the hill,
That overbrows the lonely vale.

O'er the bare upland, and away
Through the long reach of desert woods,
The embracing sunbeams chastely play,
And gladden these deep solitudes.

Where, twisted round the barren oak,
The summer vine in beauty clung,
And summer winds the stillness broke,
The crystal icicle is hung.

Where, from their frozen urns, mute springs
Pour out the river's gradual tide,
Shrilly the skater's iron rings,
And voices fill the woodland side.

Alas! how changed from the fair scene,
When birds sang out their mellow lay,
And winds were soft, and woods were green,
And the song ceased not with the day!

But still wild music is abroad,
Pale, desert woods! within your crowd;
And gathering winds, in hoarse accord,
Amid the vocal reeds pipe loud.

Chill airs and wintry winds! my ear
Has grown familiar with your song;
I hear it in the opening year,
I listen, and it cheers me long.

HYMN OF THE MORAVIAN NUNS OF BETHLEHEM

AT THE CONSECRATION OF PULASKI'S BANNER

When the dying flame of day
Through the chancel shot its ray,
Far the glimmering tapers shed
Faint light on the cowled head;
And the censer burning swung,
Where, before the altar, hung
The crimson banner, that with prayer
Had been consecrated there.
And the nuns' sweet hymn was heard the while,
Sung low, in the dim, mysterious aisle.

"Take thy banner! May it wave
Proudly o'er the good and brave;
When the battle's distant wail
Breaks the sabbath of our vale.
When the clarion's music thrills
To the hearts of these lone hills,
When the spear in conflict shakes,
And the strong lance shivering breaks.

"Take thy banner! and, beneath
The battle-cloud's encircling wreath,
Guard it, till our homes are free!
Guard it! God will prosper thee!
In the dark and trying hour,
In the breaking forth of power,
In the rush of steeds and men,
His right hand will shield thee then.

"Take thy banner! But when night
Closes round the ghastly fight,
If the vanquished warrior bow,
Spare him! By our holy vow,
By our prayers and many tears,
By the mercy that endears,
Spare him! he our love hath shared!
Spare him! as thou wouldst be spared!

"Take thy banner! and if e'er
Thou shouldst press the soldier's bier,
And the muffled drum should beat

To the tread of mournful feet,
Then this crimson flag shall be
Martial cloak and shroud for thee."

The warrior took that banner proud,
And it was his martial cloak and shroud!

SUNRISE ON THE HILLS

I stood upon the hills, when heaven's wide arch
Was glorious with the sun's returning march,
And woods were brightened, and soft gales
Went forth to kiss the sun-clad vales.
The clouds were far beneath me; bathed in light,
They gathered mid-way round the wooded height,
And, in their fading glory, shone
Like hosts in battle overthrown.
As many a pinnacle, with shifting glance.
Through the gray mist thrust up its shattered lance,
And rocking on the cliff was left
The dark pine blasted, bare, and cleft.
The veil of cloud was lifted, and below
Glowed the rich valley, and the river's flow
Was darkened by the forest's shade,
Or glistened in the white cascade;
Where upward, in the mellow blush of day,
The noisy bittern wheeled his spiral way.

I heard the distant waters dash,
I saw the current whirl and flash,
And richly, by the blue lake's silver beach,
The woods were bending with a silent reach.
Then o'er the vale, with gentle swell,
The music of the village bell
Came sweetly to the echo-giving hills;
And the wild horn, whose voice the woodland fills,
Was ringing to the merry shout,
That faint and far the glen sent out,
Where, answering to the sudden shot, thin smoke,
Through thick-leaved branches, from the dingle broke.

If thou art worn and hard beset
With sorrows, that thou wouldst forget,
If thou wouldst read a lesson, that will keep
Thy heart from fainting and thy soul from sleep,
Go to the woods and hills! No tears

Dim the sweet look that Nature wears.

THE SPIRIT OF POETRY

There is a quiet spirit in these woods,
That dwells where'er the gentle south-wind blows;
Where, underneath the white-thorn, in the glade,
The wild flowers bloom, or, kissing the soft air,
The leaves above their sunny palms outspread.
With what a tender and impassioned voice
It fills the nice and delicate ear of thought,
When the fast ushering star of morning comes
O'er-riding the gray hills with golden scarf;
Or when the cowled and dusky-sandaled Eve,
In mourning weeds, from out the western gate,
Departs with silent pace! That spirit moves
In the green valley, where the silver brook,
From its full laver, pours the white cascade;
And, babbling low amid the tangled woods,
Slips down through moss-grown stones with endless laughter.
And frequent, on the everlasting hills,
Its feet go forth, when it doth wrap itself
In all the dark embroidery of the storm,
And shouts the stern, strong wind. And here, amid
The silent majesty of these deep woods,
Its presence shall uplift thy thoughts from earth,
As to the sunshine and the pure, bright air
Their tops the green trees lift. Hence gifted bards
Have ever loved the calm and quiet shades.
For them there was an eloquent voice in all
The sylvan pomp of woods, the golden sun,
The flowers, the leaves, the river on its way,
Blue skies, and silver clouds, and gentle winds,
The swelling upland, where the sidelong sun
Aslant the wooded slope, at evening, goes,
Groves, through whose broken roof the sky looks in,
Mountain, and shattered cliff, and sunny vale,
The distant lake, fountains, and mighty trees,
In many a lazy syllable, repeating
Their old poetic legends to the wind.

And this is the sweet spirit, that doth fill
The world; and, in these wayward days of youth,
My busy fancy oft embodies it,
As a bright image of the light and beauty
That dwell in nature; of the heavenly forms

We worship in our dreams, and the soft hues
That stain the wild bird's wing, and flush the clouds
When the sun sets. Within her tender eye
The heaven of April, with its changing light,
And when it wears the blue of May, is hung,
And on her lip the rich, red rose. Her hair
Is like the summer tresses of the trees,
When twilight makes them brown, and on her cheek
Blushes the richness of an autumn sky,
With ever-shifting beauty. Then her breath,
It is so like the gentle air of Spring,
As, front the morning's dewy flowers, it comes
Full of their fragrance, that it is a joy
To have it round us, and her silver voice
Is the rich music of a summer bird,
Heard in the still night, with its passionate cadence.

BURIAL OF THE MINNISINK

On sunny slope and beechen swell,
The shadowed light of evening fell;
And, where the maple's leaf was brown,
With soft and silent lapse came down,
The glory, that the wood receives,
At sunset, in its golden leaves.

Far upward in the mellow light
Rose the blue hills. One cloud of white,
Around a far uplifted cone,
In the warm blush of evening shone;
An image of the silver lakes,
By which the Indian's soul awakes.

But soon a funeral hymn was heard
Where the soft breath of evening stirred
The tall, gray forest; and a band
Of stern in heart, and strong in hand,
Came winding down beside the wave,
To lay the red chief in his grave.

They sang, that by his native bowers
He stood, in the last moon of flowers,
And thirty snows had not yet shed
Their glory on the warrior's head;
But, as the summer fruit decays,
So died he in those naked days.

A dark cloak of the roebuck's skin
Covered the warrior, and within
Its heavy folds the weapons, made
For the hard toils of war, were laid;
The cuirass, woven of plaited reeds,
And the broad belt of shells and beads.

Before, a dark-haired virgin train
Chanted the death dirge of the slain;
Behind, the long procession came
Of hoary men and chiefs of fame,
With heavy hearts, and eyes of grief,
Leading the war-horse of their chief.

Stripped of his proud and martial dress,
Uncurbed, unreined, and riderless,
With darting eye, and nostril spread,
And heavy and impatient tread,
He came; and oft that eye so proud
Asked for his rider in the crowd.

They buried the dark chief; they freed
Beside the grave his battle steed;
And swift an arrow cleaved its way
To his stern heart! One piercing neigh
Arose, and, on the dead man's plain,
The rider grasps his steed again.

L' ENVOI

Ye voices, that arose
After the Evening's close,
And whispered to my restless heart repose!

Go, breathe it in the ear
Of all who doubt and fear,
And say to them, "Be of good cheer!"

Ye sounds, so low and calm,
That in the groves of balm
Seemed to me like an angel's psalm!

Go, mingle yet once more
With the perpetual roar
Of the pine forest dark and hoar!

Tongues of the dead, not lost
But speaking from deaths frost,
Like fiery tongues at Pentecost!

Glimmer, as funeral lamps,
Amid the chills and damps
Of the vast plain where Death encamps!

THE SKELETON IN ARMOR

"Speak! speak I thou fearful guest
Who, with thy hollow breast
Still in rude armor drest,
Comest to daunt me!
Wrapt not in Eastern balms,
Bat with thy fleshless palms
Stretched, as if asking alms,
Why dost thou haunt me?"

Then, from those cavernous eyes
Pale flashes seemed to rise,
As when the Northern skies
Gleam in December;
And, like the water's flow
Under December's snow,
Came a dull voice of woe
From the heart's chamber.

"I was a Viking old!
My deeds, though manifold,
No Skald in song has told,
No Saga taught thee!
Take heed, that in thy verse
Thou dost the tale rehearse,
Else dread a dead man's curse;
For this I sought thee.

"Far in the Northern Land,
By the wild Baltic's strand,
I, with my childish hand,
Tamed the gerfalcon;
And, with my skates fast-bound,
Skimmed the half-frozen Sound,

That the poor whimpering hound
Trembled to walk on.

"Oft to his frozen lair
Tracked I the grisly bear,
While from my path the hare
Fled like a shadow;
Oft through the forest dark
Followed the were-wolf's bark,
Until the soaring lark
Sang from the meadow.

"But when I older grew,
Joining a corsair's crew,
O'er the dark sea I flew
With the marauders.
Wild was the life we led;
Many the souls that sped,
Many the hearts that bled,
By our stern orders.

"Many a wassail-bout
Wore the long Winter out;
Often our midnight shout
Set the cocks crowing,
As we the Berserk's tale
Measured in cups of ale,
Draining the oaken pail,
Filled to o'erflowing.

"Once as I told in glee
Tales of the stormy sea,
Soft eyes did gaze on me,
Burning yet tender;
And as the white stars shine
On the dark Norway pine,
On that dark heart of mine
Fell their soft splendor.

"I wooed the blue-eyed maid,
Yielding, yet half afraid,
And in the forest's shade
Our vows were plighted.
Under its loosened vest
Fluttered her little breast
Like birds within their nest
By the hawk frighted.

"Bright in her father's hall
Shields gleamed upon the wall,
Loud sang the minstrels all,
Chanting his glory;
When of old Hildebrand
I asked his daughter's hand,
Mute did the minstrels stand
To hear my story.

"While the brown ale he quaffed,
Loud then the champion laughed,
And as the wind-gusts waft
The sea-foam brightly,
So the loud laugh of scorn,
Out of those lips unshorn,
From the deep drinking-horn
Blew the foam lightly.

"She was a Prince's child,
I but a Viking wild,
And though she blushed and smiled,
I was discarded!
Should not the dove so white
Follow the sea-mew's flight,
Why did they leave that night
Her nest unguarded?

"Scarce had I put to sea,
Bearing the maid with me,
Fairest of all was she
Among the Norsemen!
When on the white sea-strand,
Waving his armed hand,
Saw we old Hildebrand,
With twenty horsemen.

"Then launched they to the blast,
Bent like a reed each mast,
Yet we were gaining fast,
When the wind failed us;
And with a sudden flaw
Came round the gusty Skaw,
So that our foe we saw
Laugh as he hailed us.

"And as to catch the gale
Round veered the flapping sail,
Death I was the helmsman's hail,

Death without quarter!
Mid-ships with iron keel
Struck we her ribs of steel
Down her black hulk did reel
Through the black water!

"As with his wings aslant,
Sails the fierce cormorant,
Seeking some rocky haunt
With his prey laden,
So toward the open main,
Beating to sea again,
Through the wild hurricane,
Bore I the maiden.

"Three weeks we westward bore,
And when the storm was o'er,
Cloud-like we saw the shore
Stretching to leeward;
There for my lady's bower
Built I the lofty tower,
Which, to this very hour,
Stands looking seaward.

"There lived we many years;
Time dried the maiden's tears
She had forgot her fears,
She was a mother.
Death closed her mild blue eyes,
Under that tower she lies;
Ne'er shall the sun arise
On such another!

"Still grew my bosom then.
Still as a stagnant fen!
Hateful to me were men,
The sunlight hateful!
In the vast forest here,
Clad in my warlike gear,
Fell I upon my spear,
O, death was grateful!

"Thus, seamed with many scars,
Bursting these prison bars,
Up to its native stars
My soul ascended!
There from the flowing bowl
Deep drinks the warrior's soul,

Skoal! to the Northland! skoal!"
Thus the tale ended.

THE WRECK OF THE HESPERUS

It was the schooner Hesperus,
That sailed the wintry sea;
And the skipper had taken his little daughter,
To bear him company.

Blue were her eyes as the fairy-flax,
Her cheeks like the dawn of day,
And her bosom white as the hawthorn buds,
That ope in the month of May.

The skipper he stood beside the helm,
His pipe was in his month,
And he watched how the veering flaw did blow
The smoke now West, now South.

Then up and spake an old Sailor,
Had sailed to the Spanish Main,
"I pray thee, put into yonder port,
For I fear a hurricane.

"Last night, the moon had a golden ring,
And to-night no moon we see!"
The skipper, he blew a whiff from his pipe,
And a scornful laugh laughed he.

Colder and louder blew the wind,
A gale from the Northeast.
The snow fell hissing in the brine,
And the billows frothed like yeast.

Down came the storm, and smote amain
The vessel in its strength;
She shuddered and paused, like a frighted steed,
Then leaped her cable's length.

"Come hither! come hither! my little daughter,
And do not tremble so;
For I can weather the roughest gale
That ever wind did blow."

He wrapped her warm in his seaman's coat
Against the stinging blast;
He cut a rope from a broken spar,
And bound her to the mast.

"O father! I hear the church-bells ring,
O say, what may it be?"
"'Tis a fog-bell on a rock-bound coast!"—
And he steered for the open sea.

"O father! I hear the sound of guns,
O say, what may it be?"
"Some ship in distress, that cannot live
In such an angry sea!"

"O father! I see a gleaming light
O say, what may it be?"
But the father answered never a word,
A frozen corpse was he.

Lashed to the helm, all stiff and stark,
With his face turned to the skies,
The lantern gleamed through the gleaming snow
On his fixed and glassy eyes.

Then the maiden clasped her hands and prayed
That saved she might be;
And she thought of Christ, who stilled the wave,
On the Lake of Galilee.

And fast through the midnight dark and drear,
Through the whistling sleet and snow,
Like a sheeted ghost, the vessel swept
Tow'rds the reef of Norman's Woe.

And ever the fitful gusts between
A sound came from the land;
It was the sound of the trampling surf
On the rocks and the hard sea-sand.

The breakers were right beneath her bows,
She drifted a dreary wreck,
And a whooping billow swept the crew
Like icicles from her deck.

She struck where the white and fleecy waves
Looked soft as carded wool,
But the cruel rocks, they gored her side

Like the horns of an angry bull.

Her rattling shrouds, all sheathed in ice,
With the masts went by the board;
Like a vessel of glass, she stove and sank,
Ho! ho! the breakers roared!

At daybreak, on the bleak sea-beach,
A fisherman stood aghast,
To see the form of a maiden fair,
Lashed close to a drifting mast.

The salt sea was frozen on her breast,
The salt tears in her eyes;
And he saw her hair, like the brown sea-weed,
On the billows fall and rise.

Such was the wreck of the Hesperus,
In the midnight and the snow!
Christ save us all from a death like this,
On the reef of Norman's Woe!

THE VILLAGE BLACKSMITH

Under a spreading chestnut-tree
The village smithy stands;
The smith, a mighty man is he,
With large and sinewy hands;
And the muscles of his brawny arms
Are strong as iron bands.

His hair is crisp, and black, and long,
His face is like the tan;
His brow is wet with honest sweat,
He earns whate'er he can,
And looks the whole world in the face,
For he owes not any man.

Week in, week out, from morn till night,
You can hear his bellows blow;
You can hear him swing his heavy sledge,
With measured beat and slow,
Like a sexton ringing the village bell,
When the evening sun is low.

And children coming home from school

Look in at the open door;
They love to see the flaming forge,
And bear the bellows roar,
And catch the burning sparks that fly
Like chaff from a threshing-floor.

He goes on Sunday to the church,
And sits among his boys;
He hears the parson pray and preach,
He hears his daughter's voice,
Singing in the village choir,
And it makes his heart rejoice.

It sounds to him like her mother's voice,
Singing in Paradise!
He needs must think of her once more,
How in the grave she lies;
And with his hard, rough hand he wipes
A tear out of his eyes.

Toiling,—rejoicing,—sorrowing,
Onward through life he goes;
Each morning sees some task begin,
Each evening sees it close
Something attempted, something done,
Has earned a night's repose.

Thanks, thanks to thee, my worthy friend,
For the lesson thou hast taught!
Thus at the flaming forge of life
Our fortunes must be wrought;
Thus on its sounding anvil shaped
Each burning deed and thought.

ENDYMION

The rising moon has hid the stars;
Her level rays, like golden bars,
Lie on the landscape green,
With shadows brown between.

And silver white the river gleams,
As if Diana, in her dreams,
Had dropt her silver bow
Upon the meadows low.

On such a tranquil night as this,
She woke Endymion with a kiss,
When, sleeping in the grove,
He dreamed not of her love.

Like Dian's kiss, unasked, unsought,
Love gives itself, but is not bought;
Nor voice, nor sound betrays
Its deep, impassioned gaze.

It comes,—the beautiful, the free,
The crown of all humanity,—
In silence and alone
To seek the elected one.

It lifts the boughs, whose shadows deep
Are Life's oblivion, the soul's sleep,
And kisses the closed eyes
Of him, who slumbering lies.

O weary hearts! O slumbering eyes!
O drooping souls, whose destinies
Are fraught with fear and pain,
Ye shall be loved again!

No one is so accursed by fate,
No one so utterly desolate,
But some heart, though unknown,
Responds unto his own.

Responds,—as if with unseen wings,
An angel touched its quivering strings;
And whispers, in its song,
"'Where hast thou stayed so long?"

IT IS NOT ALWAYS MAY

No hay pajaros en los nidos de antano.
Spanish Proverb

The sun is bright,—the air is clear,
The darting swallows soar and sing.
And from the stately elms I hear
The bluebird prophesying Spring.

So blue you winding river flows,

It seems an outlet from the sky,
Where waiting till the west-wind blows,
The freighted clouds at anchor lie.

All things are new;—the buds, the leaves,
That gild the elm-tree's nodding crest,
And even the nest beneath the eaves;—
There are no birds in last year's nest!

All things rejoice in youth and love,
The fulness of their first delight!
And learn from the soft heavens above
The melting tenderness of night.

Maiden, that read'st this simple rhyme,
Enjoy thy youth, it will not stay;
Enjoy the fragrance of thy prime,
For oh, it is not always May!

Enjoy the Spring of Love and Youth,
To some good angel leave the rest;
For Time will teach thee soon the truth,
There are no birds in last year's nest!

THE RAINY DAY

The day is cold, and dark, and dreary
It rains, and the wind is never weary;
The vine still clings to the mouldering wall,
But at every gust the dead leaves fall,
And the day is dark and dreary.

My life is cold, and dark, and dreary;
It rains, and the wind is never weary;
My thoughts still cling to the mouldering Past,
But the hopes of youth fall thick in the blast,
And the days are dark and dreary.

Be still, sad heart! and cease repining;
Behind the clouds is the sun still shining;
Thy fate is the common fate of all,
Into each life some rain must fall,
Some days must be dark and dreary.

GOD'S-ACRE

I like that ancient Saxon phrase, which calls
The burial-ground God's-Acre! It is just;
It consecrates each grave within its walls,
And breathes a benison o'er the sleeping dust.

God's-Acre! Yes, that blessed name imparts
Comfort to those, who in the grave have sown
The seed that they had garnered in their hearts,
Their bread of life, alas! no more their own.

Into its furrows shall we all be cast,
In the sure faith, that we shall rise again
At the great harvest, when the archangel's blast
Shall winnow, like a fan, the chaff and grain.

Then shall the good stand in immortal bloom,
In the fair gardens of that second birth;
And each bright blossom mingle its perfume
With that of flowers, which never bloomed on earth.

With thy rude ploughshare, Death, turn up the sod,
And spread the furrow for the seed we sow;
This is the field and Acre of our God,
This is the place where human harvests grow!

TO THE RIVER CHARLES

River! that in silence windest
Through the meadows, bright and free,
Till at length thy rest thou findest
In the bosom of the sea!

Four long years of mingled feeling,
Half in rest, and half in strife,
I have seen thy waters stealing
Onward, like the stream of life.

Thou hast taught me, Silent River!
Many a lesson, deep and long;
Thou hast been a generous giver;
I can give thee but a song.

Oft in sadness and in illness,
I have watched thy current glide,

Till the beauty of its stillness
Overflowed me, like a tide.

And in better hours and brighter,
When I saw thy waters gleam,
I have felt my heart beat lighter,
And leap onward with thy stream.

Not for this alone I love thee,
Nor because thy waves of blue
From celestial seas above thee
Take their own celestial hue.

Where yon shadowy woodlands hide thee,
And thy waters disappear,
Friends I love have dwelt beside thee,
And have made thy margin dear.

More than this;—thy name reminds me
Of three friends, all true and tried;
And that name, like magic, binds me
Closer, closer to thy side.

Friends my soul with joy remembers!
How like quivering flames they start,
When I fan the living embers
On the hearth-stone of my heart!

'T is for this, thou Silent River!
That my spirit leans to thee;
Thou hast been a generous giver,
Take this idle song from me.

BLIND BARTIMEUS

Blind Bartimeus at the gates
Of Jericho in darkness waits;
He hears the crowd;--he hears a breath
Say, "It is Christ of Nazareth!"
And calls, in tones of agony,
'Ιησου, ἐλξησὸν με!

The thronging multitudes increase;
Blind Bartimeus, hold thy peace!
But still, above the noisy crowd,
The beggar's cry is shrill and loud;

Until they say, "He calleth thee!"
Θαρσει ζγειραι , φωνει σε!

Then saith the Christ, as silent stands
The crowd, "What wilt thou at my hands?"
And he replies, "Oh, give me light!
Rabbi, restore the blind man's sight."
And Jesus answers, "Υπαγε'
'Η πιστις σου σεσωκε σε!

Ye that have eyes, yet cannot see,
In darkness and in misery,
Recall those mighty Voices Three,
'Ιησου, ξλξησδν με!
Θαρσει ξγειραι, υπαγε!
'Η πιστις σου σεσωκε σε!

THE GOBLET OF LIFE

Filled is Life's goblet to the brim;
And though my eyes with tears are dim,
I see its sparkling bubbles swim,
And chant a melancholy hymn
With solemn voice and slow.

No purple flowers,—no garlands green,
Conceal the goblet's shade or sheen,
Nor maddening draughts of Hippocrene,
Like gleams of sunshine, flash between
Thick leaves of mistletoe.

This goblet, wrought with curious art,
Is filled with waters, that upstart,
When the deep fountains of the heart,
By strong convulsions rent apart,
Are running all to waste.

And as it mantling passes round,
With fennel is it wreathed and crowned,
Whose seed and foliage sun-imbrowned
Are in its waters steeped and drowned,
And give a bitter taste.

Above the lowly plants it towers,
The fennel, with its yellow flowers,
And in an earlier age than ours

Was gifted with the wondrous powers,
Lost vision to restore.

It gave new strength, and fearless mood;
And gladiators, fierce and rude,
Mingled it in their daily food;
And he who battled and subdued,
A wreath of fennel wore.

Then in Life's goblet freely press,
The leaves that give it bitterness,
Nor prize the colored waters less,
For in thy darkness and distress
New light and strength they give!

And he who has not learned to know
How false its sparkling bubbles show,
How bitter are the drops of woe,
With which its brim may overflow,
He has not learned to live.

The prayer of Ajax was for light;
Through all that dark and desperate fight
The blackness of that noonday night
He asked but the return of sight,
To see his foeman's face.

Let our unceasing, earnest prayer
Be, too, for light,—for strength to bear
Our portion of the weight of care,
That crushes into dumb despair
One half the human race.

O suffering, sad humanity!
O ye afflicted one; who lie
Steeped to the lips in misery,
Longing, and yet afraid to die,
Patient, though sorely tried!

I pledge you in this cup of grief,
Where floats the fennel's bitter leaf!
The Battle of our Life is brief
The alarm,—the struggle,—the relief,
Then sleep we side by side.

MAIDENHOOD

Maiden! with the meek, brown eyes,
In whose orbs a shadow lies
Like the dusk in evening skies!

Thou whose locks outshine the sun,
Golden tresses, wreathed in one,
As the braided streamlets run!

Standing, with reluctant feet,
Where the brook and river meet,
Womanhood and childhood fleet!

Gazing, with a timid glance,
On the brooklet's swift advance,
On the river's broad expanse!

Deep and still, that gliding stream
Beautiful to thee must seem,
As the river of a dream.

Then why pause with indecision,
When bright angels in thy vision
Beckon thee to fields Elysian?

Seest thou shadows sailing by,
As the dove, with startled eye,
Sees the falcon's shadow fly?

Hearest thou voices on the shore,
That our ears perceive no more,
Deafened by the cataract's roar?

O, thou child of many prayers!
Life hath quicksands,—Life hath snares
Care and age come unawares!

Like the swell of some sweet tune,
Morning rises into noon,
May glides onward into June.

Childhood is the bough, where slumbered
Birds and blossoms many-numbered;—
Age, that bough with snows encumbered.

Gather, then, each flower that grows,
When the young heart overflows,
To embalm that tent of snows.

Bear a lily in thy hand;
Gates of brass cannot withstand
One touch of that magic wand.

Bear through sorrow, wrong, and ruth,
In thy heart the dew of youth,
On thy lips the smile of truth!

O, that dew, like balm, shall steal
Into wounds that cannot heal,
Even as sleep our eyes doth seal;

And that smile, like sunshine, dart
Into many a sunless heart,
For a smile of God thou art.

EXCELSIOR

The shades of night were falling fast,
As through an Alpine village passed
A youth, who bore, 'mid snow and ice,
A banner with the strange device,
Excelsior!

His brow was sad; his eye beneath,
Flashed like a falchion from its sheath,
And like a silver clarion rung
The accents of that unknown tongue,
Excelsior!

In happy homes he saw the light
Of household fires gleam warm and bright;
Above, the spectral glaciers shone,
And from his lips escaped a groan,
Excelsior!

"Try not the Pass!" the old man said:
"Dark lowers the tempest overhead,
The roaring torrent is deep and wide!
And loud that clarion voice replied,
Excelsior!

"Oh stay," the maiden said, "and rest
Thy weary head upon this breast!"
A tear stood in his bright blue eye,

But still he answered, with a sigh,
Excelsior!

"Beware the pine-tree's withered branch!
Beware the awful avalanche!"
This was the peasant's last Good-night,
A voice replied, far up the height,
Excelsior!

At break of day, as heavenward
The pious monks of Saint Bernard
Uttered the oft-repeated prayer,
A voice cried through the startled air,
Excelsior!

A traveller, by the faithful hound,
Half-buried in the snow was found,
Still grasping in his hand of ice
That banner with the strange device,
Excelsior!

There in the twilight cold and gray,
Lifeless, but beautiful, he lay,
And from the sky, serene and far,
A voice fell, like a falling star,
Excelsior!

POEMS ON SLAVERY

The following poems, with one exception, were written at sea, in the latter part of October, 1842. I had not then heard of Dr. Channing's death. Since that event, the poem addressed to him is no longer appropriate. I have decided, however, to let it remain as it was written, in testimony of my admiration for a great and good man.

TO WILLIAM E. CHANNING

The pages of thy book I read,
And as I closed each one,
My heart, responding, ever said,
"Servant of God! well done!"

Well done! Thy words are great and bold;
At times they seem to me,
Like Luther's, in the days of old,
Half-battles for the free.

Go on, until this land revokes
The old and chartered Lie,
The feudal curse, whose whips and yokes
Insult humanity.

A voice is ever at thy side
Speaking in tones of might,
Like the prophetic voice, that cried
To John in Patmos, "Write!"

Write! and tell out this bloody tale;
Record this dire eclipse,
This Day of Wrath, this Endless Wail,
This dread Apocalypse!

THE SLAVE'S DREAM

Beside the ungathered rice he lay,
His sickle in his hand;
His breast was bare, his matted hair
Was buried in the sand.
Again, in the mist and shadow of sleep,
He saw his Native Land.

Wide through the landscape of his dreams
The lordly Niger flowed;
Beneath the palm-trees on the plain
Once more a king he strode;
And heard the tinkling caravans
Descend the mountain-road.

He saw once more his dark-eyed queen
Among her children stand;
They clasped his neck, they kissed his cheeks,
They held him by the hand!—
A tear burst from the sleeper's lids
And fell into the sand.

And then at furious speed he rode
Along the Niger's bank;
His bridle-reins were golden chains,
And, with a martial clank,
At each leap he could feel his scabbard of steel
Smiting his stallion's flank.

Before him, like a blood-red flag,
The bright flamingoes flew;
From morn till night he followed their flight,
O'er plains where the tamarind grew,
Till he saw the roofs of Caffre huts,
And the ocean rose to view.

At night he heard the lion roar,
And the hyena scream,
And the river-horse, as he crushed the reeds
Beside some hidden stream;
And it passed, like a glorious roll of drums,
Through the triumph of his dream.

The forests, with their myriad tongues,
Shouted of liberty;
And the Blast of the Desert cried aloud,
With a voice so wild and free,
That he started in his sleep and smiled
At their tempestuous glee.

He did not feel the driver's whip,
Nor the burning heat of day;
For Death had illumined the Land of Sleep,
And his lifeless body lay
A worn-out fetter, that the soul
Had broken and thrown away!

THE GOOD PART

THAT SHALL NOT BE TAKEN AWAY

She dwells by Great Kenhawa's side,
In valleys green and cool;
And all her hope and all her pride
Are in the village school.

Her soul, like the transparent air
That robes the hills above,
Though not of earth, encircles there
All things with arms of love.

And thus she walks among her girls
With praise and mild rebukes;
Subduing e'en rude village churls
By her angelic looks.

She reads to them at eventide
Of One who came to save;
To cast the captive's chains aside
And liberate the slave.

And oft the blessed time foretells
When all men shall be free;
And musical, as silver bells,
Their falling chains shall be.

And following her beloved Lord,
In decent poverty,
She makes her life one sweet record
And deed of charity.

For she was rich, and gave up all
To break the iron bands
Of those who waited in her hall,
And labored in her lands.

Long since beyond the Southern Sea
Their outbound sails have sped,
While she, in meek humility,
Now earns her daily bread.

It is their prayers, which never cease,
That clothe her with such grace;
Their blessing is the light of peace
That shines upon her face.

THE SLAVE IN THE DISMAL SWAMP

In dark fens of the Dismal Swamp
The hunted Negro lay;
He saw the fire of the midnight camp,
And heard at times a horse's tramp
And a bloodhound's distant bay.

Where will-o'-the-wisps and glow-worms shine,
In bulrush and in brake;
Where waving mosses shroud the pine,
And the cedar grows, and the poisonous vine
Is spotted like the snake;

Where hardly a human foot could pass,

Or a human heart would dare,
On the quaking turf of the green morass
He crouched in the rank and tangled grass,
Like a wild beast in his lair.

A poor old slave, infirm and lame;
Great scars deformed his face;
On his forehead he bore the brand of shame,
And the rags, that hid his mangled frame,
Were the livery of disgrace.

All things above were bright and fair,
All things were glad and free;
Lithe squirrels darted here and there,
And wild birds filled the echoing air
With songs of Liberty!

On him alone was the doom of pain,
From the morning of his birth;
On him alone the curse of Cain
Fell, like a flail on the garnered grain,
And struck him to the earth!

THE SLAVE SINGING AT MIDNIGHT

Loud he sang the psalm of David!
He, a Negro and enslaved,
Sang of Israel's victory,
Sang of Zion, bright and free.

In that hour, when night is calmest,
Sang he from the Hebrew Psalmist,
In a voice so sweet and clear
That I could not choose but hear,

Songs of triumph, and ascriptions,
Such as reached the swart Egyptians,
When upon the Red Sea coast
Perished Pharaoh and his host.

And the voice of his devotion
Filled my soul with strange emotion;
For its tones by turns were glad,
Sweetly solemn, wildly sad.

Paul and Silas, in their prison,

Sang of Christ, the Lord arisen,
And an earthquake's arm of might
Broke their dungeon-gates at night.

But, alas! what holy angel
Brings the Slave this glad evangel?
And what earthquake's arm of might
Breaks his dungeon-gates at night?

THE WITNESSES

In Ocean's wide domains,
Half buried in the sands,
Lie skeletons in chains,
With shackled feet and hands.

Beyond the fall of dews,
Deeper than plummet lies,
Float ships, with all their crews,
No more to sink nor rise.

There the black Slave-ship swims,
Freighted with human forms,
Whose fettered, fleshless limbs
Are not the sport of storms.

These are the bones of Slaves;
They gleam from the abyss;
They cry, from yawning waves,
"We are the Witnesses!"

Within Earth's wide domains
Are markets for men's lives;
Their necks are galled with chains,
Their wrists are cramped with gyves.

Dead bodies, that the kite
In deserts makes its prey;
Murders, that with affright
Scare school-boys from their play!

All evil thoughts and deeds;
Anger, and lust, and pride;
The foulest, rankest weeds,
That choke Life's groaning tide!

These are the woes of Slaves;
They glare from the abyss;
They cry, from unknown graves,
"We are the Witnesses!

THE QUADROON GIRL

The Slaver in the broad lagoon
Lay moored with idle sail;
He waited for the rising moon,
And for the evening gale.

Under the shore his boat was tied,
And all her listless crew
Watched the gray alligator slide
Into the still bayou.

Odors of orange-flowers, and spice,
Reached them from time to time,
Like airs that breathe from Paradise
Upon a world of crime.

The Planter, under his roof of thatch,
Smoked thoughtfully and slow;
The Slaver's thumb was on the latch,
He seemed in haste to go.

He said, "My ship at anchor rides
In yonder broad lagoon;
I only wait the evening tides,
And the rising of the moon.

Before them, with her face upraised,
In timid attitude,
Like one half curious, half amazed,
A Quadroon maiden stood.

Her eyes were large, and full of light,
Her arms and neck were bare;
No garment she wore save a kirtle bright,
And her own long, raven hair.

And on her lips there played a smile
As holy, meek, and faint,
As lights in some cathedral aisle
The features of a saint.

"The soil is barren,—the farm is old";
The thoughtful planter said;
Then looked upon the Slaver's gold,
And then upon the maid.

His heart within him was at strife
With such accursed gains:
For he knew whose passions gave her life,
Whose blood ran in her veins.

But the voice of nature was too weak;
He took the glittering gold!
Then pale as death grew the maiden's cheek,
Her hands as icy cold.

The Slaver led her from the door,
He led her by the hand,
To be his slave and paramour
In a strange and distant land!

THE WARNING

Beware! The Israelite of old, who tore
The lion in his path,—when, poor and blind,
He saw the blessed light of heaven no more,
Shorn of his noble strength and forced to grind
In prison, and at last led forth to be
A pander to Philistine revelry,—

Upon the pillars of the temple laid
His desperate hands, and in its overthrow
Destroyed himself, and with him those who made
A cruel mockery of his sightless woe;
The poor, blind Slave, the scoff and jest of all,
Expired, and thousands perished in the fall!

There is a poor, blind Samson in this land,
Shorn of his strength and bound in bonds of steel,
Who may, in some grim revel, raise his hand,
And shake the pillars of this Commonweal,
Till the vast Temple of our liberties.
A shapeless mass of wreck and rubbish lies.

www.ingramcontent.com/pod-product-compliance
Lightning Source LLC
Chambersburg PA
CBHW060100050426
42448CB00011B/2554